THIS CANDLEWICK BOOK BELONGS TO:

_____

_____

_____

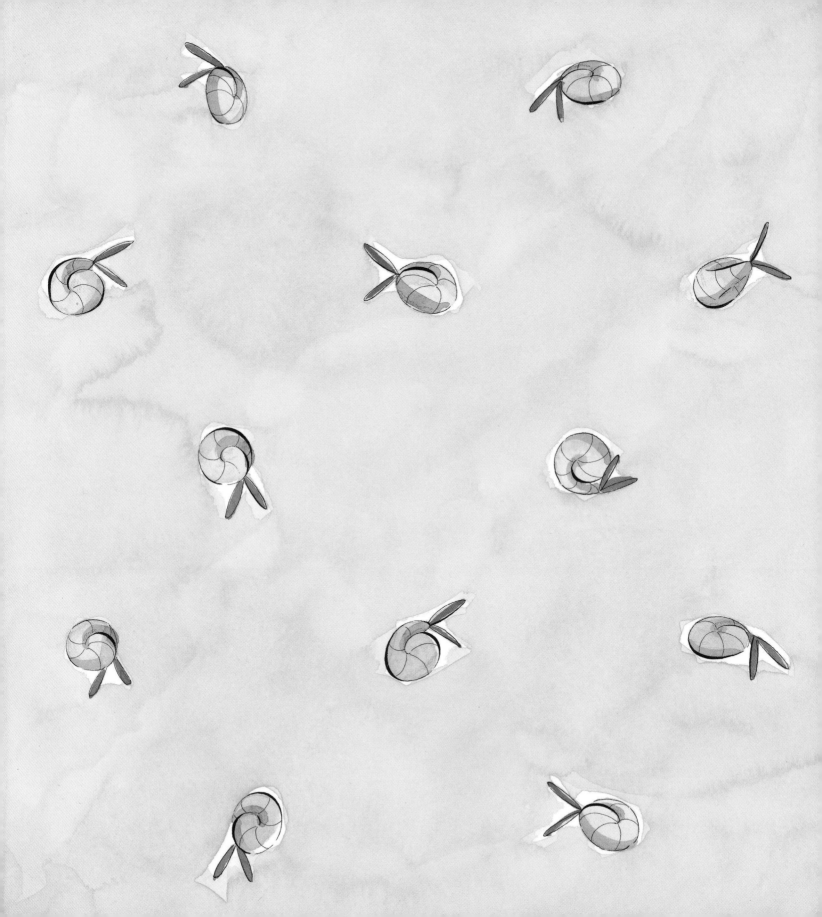

For Lucy

First paperback edition 2009

The Library of Congress has cataloged the hardcover edition as follows:

Harper, Jamie.
Miss Mingo and the first day of school / Jamie Harper. — 1st. ed.
p.   cm.
Summary: Miss Mingo helps all of the animal students in her class overcome their shyness on the
first day of school by encouraging them to share something special about themselves. Includes
facts about animals.
ISBN 978-0-7636-2410-1 (hardcover)
[1. First day of school — Juvenile fiction. 2. Teachers — Juvenile fiction. 3. Flamingos — Juvenile
fiction. 4. Animals — Juvenile fiction. 5. Schools — Juvenile fiction. 6. First day of school —
Fiction. 7. Teachers — Fiction. 8. Flamingos — Fiction. 9. Animals — Fiction. 10. Schools —
Fiction.]   I. Title.
PZ7.H23134 Mis 2006
[E] — dc22   2005055308

ISBN 978-0-7636-4134-4 (paperback)

15 16 17 CCP 10 9 8 7 6 5 4

Printed in Shenzhen, Guangdong, China

This book was typeset in Alghera.
The illustrations were done in watercolor and ink.

Candlewick Press
99 Dover Street
Somerville, Massachusetts 02144

visit us at www.candlewick.com

Miss Mingo
and the First Day of School

Jamie Harper

CANDLEWICK PRESS

The first day of school was Miss Mingo's favorite.
She couldn't wait to meet her new students.
Of course, everyone was a bit nervous,
but Miss Mingo knew just what to do.

"Let's take turns sharing something special
about ourselves," she began. "It can be anything!"
Miss Mingo smiled at her students.
No one smiled back.

"Well, then, why don't I begin?"

"I'll bet you didn't know that the food I eat keeps me in the pink," said Miss Mingo, sipping a shrimp shake. "And I always eat upside down."

A flamingo's bill is hinged at the top, allowing this bird to scoop up food in the water with its head upside down. Carotenoids, a substance in shrimp, make a flamingo's feathers pink. Without them, its feathers would turn white!

Everyone stared.

"WOW!" whispered Narwhal.

"Who knew?" muttered Giraffe.

"She's marvelous," said Hippo with a sigh.

Alligator jumped up to go next.

"I'm always losing my teeth," she declared.

"See my collection? Thank goodness
I grow new ones all the time."

An alligator can grow and lose
up to 3,000 teeth in its lifetime.

"Doesn't she know
about the tooth fairy?"
asked Koala.

"Shhhhhe
could be rich,"
said Snake.

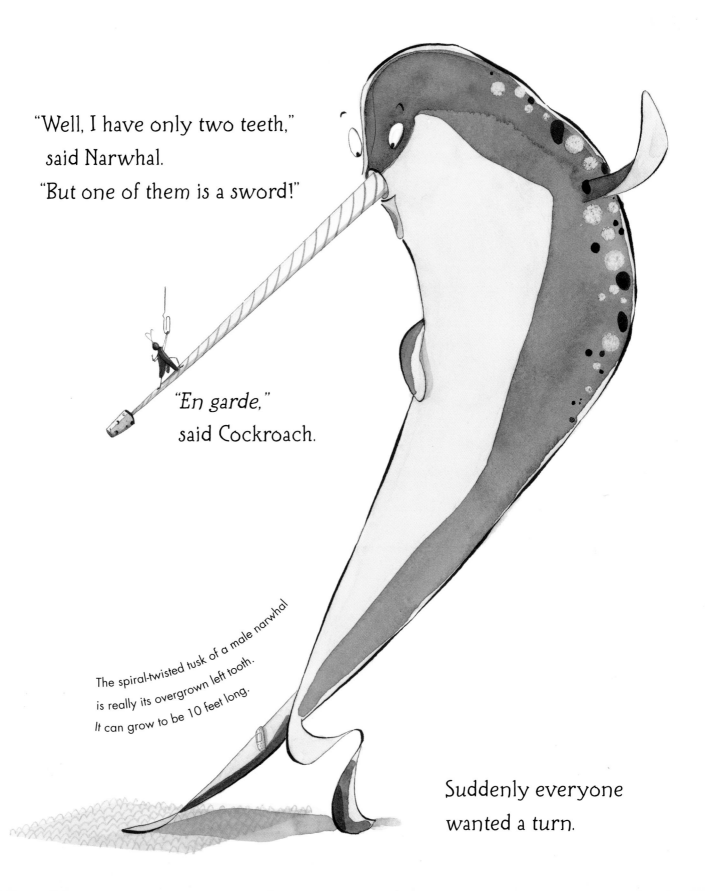

"Well, I have only two teeth,"
said Narwhal.
"But one of them is a sword!"

"En garde,"
said Cockroach.

The spiral-twisted tusk of a male narwhal
is really its overgrown left tooth.
It can grow to be 10 feet long.

Suddenly everyone
wanted a turn.

"Look what I made," Spider said proudly.
"Simply stunning!" said Miss Mingo.

An orb web spider can weave its circular web in just 30 to 45 minutes.

"Yikes! That was fast,"
said Frog.

"Well, I may be tiny, but I'm
super strong," Ant announced,
balancing a fresh pink eraser
from down below.

The wingless worker ant can
lift 50 times its own weight.

"Listen to this," Bird sang.
"I know more than a
thousand songs by heart."
Miss Mingo was tickled pink.

The male brown thrasher has the largest repertoire of all
North American birds, with more than 1,100 song types.

Koala plucked a eucalyptus leaf. "This is my favorite food," he said. "It's all I ever eat for breakfast, lunch, and dinner."

"Yuck," said Alligator. "Smells like a cough drop."

Eucalyptus leaves are a koala's only source of food and water. *Koala* is an Aboriginal word meaning "does not drink."

"When I was a baby," Panda shouted, "I was no bigger than a hot dog. See?"

A newborn panda cub is pink and blind—and 900 times smaller than its mother.

Centipede was busy buckling her boots when
Miss Mingo asked her to go next.
"My name means 'one hundred feet.' But *obviously*,
I have *way more than that*," she said, rolling her eyes.

"Check out that shoe collection," Frog said, counting.

Centipedes can have as many as 354 legs.

By snack time, the class was really warming up.

"I TASTE with my suckers,"
Octopus said with a slurp.
"Everything's yummy!"

"I HEAR with
my legs,"
said Cricket,
frowning
at Octopus.
"Could you please
eat more quietly?"

A cricket's "ears"
are flat and oval-shaped.
They are located on its front legs.

An octopus has almost 2,000 suckers.
With them, it can taste the difference
between sweet, salty, and bitter foods.

"Impressive," Miss Mingo said, laughing. "Now *that's* using your senses!"

"I SMELL with my tongue," said Snake. "Ooooooh, that cheesy popcorn sssssstinks."

Snakes flick their tongues in and out to pick up scents from the air and ground.

"Miss Mingo,
Elephant's
asleep,"
Alligator
tattled.

"Oh, how cute,"
said Miss Mingo.

"And he's sucking his trunk,"
Frog whispered. "Actually
he can breathe, smell, eat,
drink, wash, wrestle, and
trumpet with it too."

A tired elephant calf often sucks
the tip of its trunk for comfort, just
as a human baby sucks its thumb.

With lips that are about two feet wide, a hippopotamus can eat up to 100 pounds of marsh grass and other plants a day.

hippo

"MY TURN!" Hippo hollered from across the room.
He had something special for Miss Mingo.
Now she was tickled *bright* pink.
"These big, big lips aren't just great for grazing," he said
with a giggle. Everyone else giggled too.

Monkey swung down from the ceiling light.

"Talk about BIG," he boasted. "See this nose?

It'll never stop growing."

"Well, it'll never get as long as my tongue," said Giraffe.

"Now, now, let's watch our manners,"

Miss Mingo reminded the class.

But it was too late.

The male proboscis monkey's nose continues growing throughout its lifetime and may get to be 4 inches long.

A giraffe's flexible, dark purple tongue can extend to 18 inches— perfect for stripping leaves off tall trees.

"I can eat *anything*!" yelled Cockroach, chewing on a book.

"Even your own skin?" Frog challenged.

"Mine's delicious and nutritious."

Cockroaches eat almost anything, including plants, animal carcasses, paper, glue, soap— even nail clippings.

Some frogs eat their own skin as they molt, using their front legs to pull it off over their heads.

"Ugh," groaned Alligator.

"I can't watch."

"Who hasn't had a turn?" asked Miss Mingo, glancing
over at Pig. "Remember, tell us something special."
Pig thought hard for a minute. "I know," she exclaimed.
"My skin is very sensitive to the sun."
"Mercy me!" Miss Mingo said, cringing.
"Doesn't she know about sunblock?" asked Alligator.

Pigs are susceptible to sunburn.
They roll in the mud to give
their skin a protective coating.

Miss Mingo's class was full of surprises, but nothing prepared them for what came next.

"My pouch can hold lots of water," Pelican said, stepping back from the sink.
"Gallons!" croaked Frog. "Who knew?"
"Who cares?" yelled Cockroach. "Last one in is a rotten egg."

Pelicans use their pouches as nets to capture fish. The pouch can stretch to hold up to three and a half gallons of water.

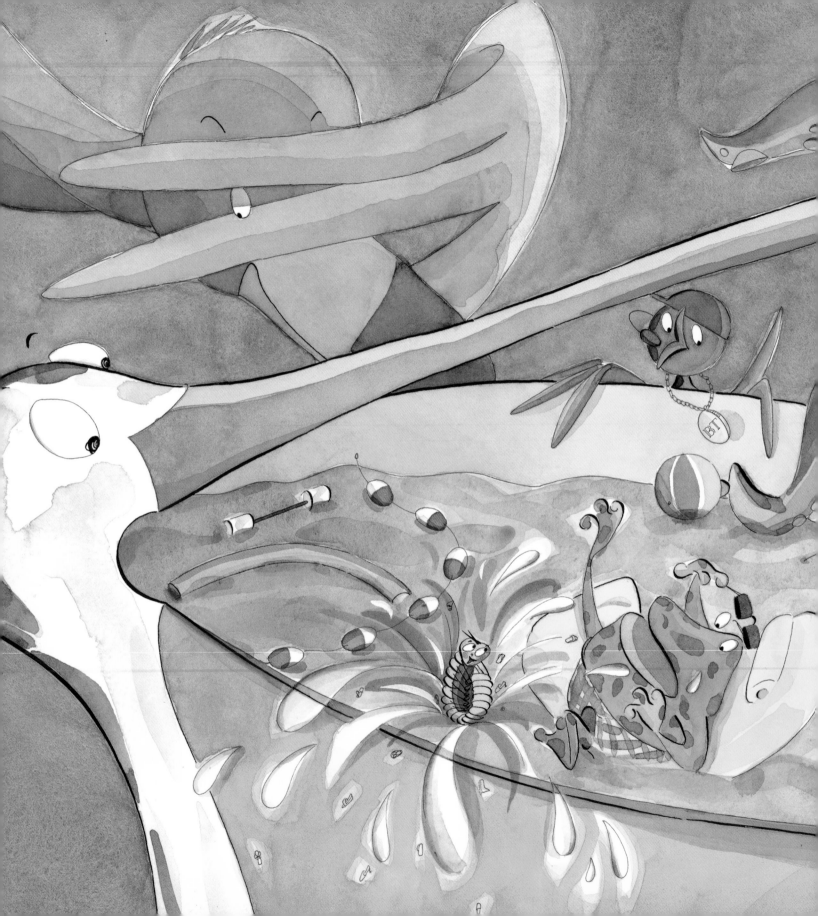

The pool party made quite a splash,
but soon it was time to dry off
and go home.
Miss Mingo was thrilled.
She had learned so many extraordinary
things about her students.

"What a fabulous year we'll have,"
she thought as she mopped up.
"What a fabulous class!"

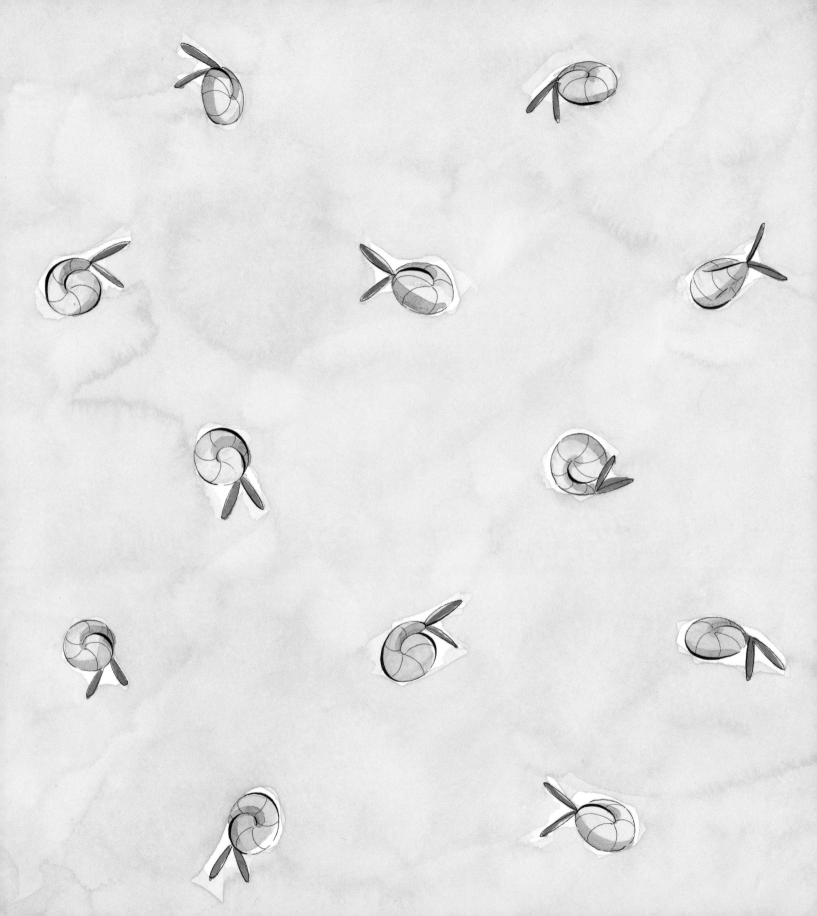

Jamie Harper is the author-illustrator of several books for children, including *Night Night, Baby Bundt* and *Splish Splash, Baby Bundt*. About *Miss Mingo and the First Day of School*, she says, "I like that this story is a blend of fiction and nonfiction, and that Miss Mingo is a funky, fun, contemporary teacher who just loves learning new things." Jamie Harper lives outside Boston, Massachusetts, with her husband and three daughters.